Financially Hopeless No More

By

Lynn Busch and Courtney Henderson

Using Money to Reshape Your Life

Financially Hopeless No More

Copyright © 2007 by Lynn Busch and Courtney Henderson

Published by Dare2Dream Books, Mustang, Oklahoma
A Division of
McCowan and Morris Publishing Company
405-642-8257

All rights reserved. No part of this book may be reproduced, stored in a retrieval system or transmitted in any form by any means, electronic, mechanical, photocopy, recording or otherwise, without the prior written permission of the author, except as provided by USA copyright law.

Printed in the United States of America by
Dare2Dream Books

Publisher's Cataloging in Publication

Busch, Lynn and Henderson, Courtney

Financially Hopeless No More

1. Christianity, 2. Finances, 3. Self-help

ISBN 0-9779688-6-3

~Acknowledgements~

We would like to thank our editor, Bev Herring, for her devotion to the book and for her encouragement. We also thank Dr. Glen Jennings, who saw the book before we did and encouraged us to write it. We thank Brandon Busch, who gave us invaluable computer support, and Courtney's husband, Owen, for his support and encouragement. Lastly, we would like to thank all of our workshop participants who gave us helpful feedback, and kept asking, "When is the book going to be finished?"

Using Money to Reshape Your Life

Table of Contents

Introduction		7
Preface		9
Chapter 1	Lynn and Courtney's Story-Then	13
Chapter 2	Lynn and Courtney's Story-Now	21
Chapter 3	Recognize that Your Present Money Behavior is not Working for You	29
Chapter 4	Make a Commitment to Educate Yourself about Money	35
Chapter 5	Now Do the Work	41
Chapter 6	Begin Applying Your Knowledge to Your Own Finances	49
Chapter 7	Goal Setting for the Future	65
Chapter 8	Taking it to the Next Level – Saving, Investing, Spending	69
Chapter 9	Beyond Financial Independence	83
Chapter 10	Becoming Debt Free	93
Conclusion		101
Appendix	Book and Tape List	103

Using Money to Reshape Your Life

~Introduction~

"Money, which represents the prose of life, and which is hardly spoken of in parlors without an apology, is, in its effects and laws, as beautiful as roses." -- Ralph Waldo Emerson

Financially Hopeless No More will help you transform your thoughts about money and change your relationship with money even if you have been fearful, frustrated, and out of control for decades. Even if you are convinced there is no hope for your financial future, this book will show you how to use money as a tool to reshape your entire life. Take this fascinating journey with authors, Lynn Busch and Courtney Henderson, who went from total failure and frustration with money to a peaceful, happy, and successful financial life.

This book will take you through the *process* of changing your relationship with money. This book offers practical, easy to implement actions that will begin to change your understanding of money and ultimately your life. You will start to experience *fun with money* almost right away!

In this book you will learn how to get out of debt, track your money, develop your own income/expense record, and develop your own spending plan. You will learn about the five accounts that will almost organize your money for you.

You will learn why money has eluded you and how implementing these principles will change you into a financially free person. Lynn and Courtney will be with you every step of the way with sage advice and fascinating insights into the world of money.

If you have struggled with money all your life and have trouble keeping your head above water, or you just want to figure out how to pay your bills without developing a stress disorder, *Financially Hopeless No More* is your key to a new life.

~*Preface*~

This book is not a technical manual or an investment guide. This book is about moving from point A to point B. It was written by two women who challenged and supported each other along the way to their financial freedom. It is the authors' hope that their struggles and victories will make your own money journey from hopelessness to freedom easier and more fun.

Courtney: "I had been in counseling for about three years and had come face to face with the fact that money was a very emotional issue with me. I had reached a point where I had to make a choice: either stop the inner work and tell myself I was finished, or open the door to this last closed room called "money." I still don't know why I chose to open the door, but it changed my entire life."

Lynn: "When Courtney began to investigate the emotional ties surrounding money, my ears perked up. As a counselor I had been interested in the study of money and its impact on creativity, relationships, and societal systems. I had seen for a long time before I became a counselor that money had tremendous power for good or evil in a person's life. I also knew that most people were afraid of unlocking this mysterious force. So when Courtney introduced the subject, I seized the opportunity to go further. At this point I had been divorced for five years and things had begun to settle. I was ready to go further with my own personal understanding of the role money played in my life. Here was someone who would be willing to take this money journey with me. And, she would be able to be objective and analytical—two of my own personal characteristics."

We started by reading books on all aspects of money. We read them a chapter at a time and lingered for as long as we wished over any passages that interested us. We read our chapters independently and then met by phone three mornings a week to discuss and process the information together. We did every suggested exercise in every book we read, and this proved to be invaluable. That is why it took us so long to read the books. We were trying to absorb everything the author had to say. Some of the exercises we did together, and some we did as homework. Some books we read more than once—and talked about more than once. Our goal was to get a *deep* understanding and to translate that understanding into new behaviors in our lives.

If you choose to read books about money using the three mornings a week structure, you should know that it is not enough to just read about the subject. It is not even enough to "read and merely discuss the information." It is only enough when you become so fully immersed in the process that you feel you are rewiring your brain. That is exactly what you *are* doing—rewiring your brain. You will be overcoming years—even generations—of contrary and outdated information. The first two chapters in the book are our own personal stories of what this immersion process has done in our lives. Your money journey will never really end, but it will become, believe it or not, one of the most exciting trips you will ever take.

Our purpose is not to sugar coat this process. It is to provide a means by which anyone can take control of his or her own financial destiny. We are not going to tell you that there is a way to get your finances organized in thirty minutes. We are not going to tell you that you can accomplish life-changing results "in your spare time" or "on your lunch hour." We *are* going to tell you some of the things we have learned along the way that we hope will be useful in your own money journey. We *are* going to tell you that this journey is one of the most fulfilling things we've ever done. We *are* going to tell you the journey has been worth all the effort to us.

What is financial freedom worth to you? If it seems to be too much trouble, or if it seems like it will take too long, take a leap of faith. Your financial freedom will be worth it. For now, just know that if we could do it, anyone can, and we will be right here with you to cheer you on your way.

Using Money to Reshape Your Life

~Chapter 1~
Lynn and Courtney's Story-Then

"I should not talk so much about myself if there were anybody else whom I knew as well." -- Henry David Thoreau

Lynn's Story – Then

Three years ago I was totally overwhelmed by the chaos in my financial affairs. Every horrible thing you can imagine had happened, and it *wasn't over yet*. At the age of fifty-two, I was divorced after 24 years of marriage. This occurred six months after a Chapter Seven bankruptcy, so there was not a fat settlement.

A typical month went like this. I was usually late for my rent. My credit cards were maxed out, and my bills were paid at the last minute with money I hoped to have soon. I often had to borrow money until the next check. Worst of all, my concept of the future was non-existent. I was still financially tied to the past because I had to pay debts left over from a former business. I was even paying medical expenses my father had incurred before his death four years ago. I felt overwhelmed, helpless, angry, alone, and just generally inadequate to face this gargantuan task. My financial life had become a black hole, and I used up all my energy trying to stay afloat. I did not know where to begin to clean up this mess. In fact it was so huge I didn't think I could approach a solution without a magical infusion of significant wealth.

At my age I was not looking for this magic to arrive on a white horse. But, in the past that was my concept of how a woman got wealth—either from daddy or a husband. Early on, I figured out that daddy wasn't going to hold on to his wealth long enough to transfer it to me. So that left the husband option. From the beginning of the relationship with my husband, the major issue was money. This was the main topic of concern that overrode all other issues in our marriage. We were self-destructive with our money. We got ourselves into many situations that were not profitable. We almost looked for ways to lose money. In spite of this, our income stream was large enough to keep us afloat. In fact it financed our stupidity.

The years leading up to the divorce had given the word "devastation" a new meaning in my life. In 1984 my husband and I were financially well off, and it seemed that the ensuing years would be prosperous. In 1985, a series of events took place that began the unraveling of our financial and personal lives. While we were busy planning our retirement in New Mexico, several things happened all at once from which we never recovered financially. Part of this was because we did not have good information and made some unfortunate choices, but mostly it was because we could not come together as a team to deal with our finances. While the inability to work as a financial team was a problem early in our marriage, it finally became insurmountable.

I thought that once we were divorced my financial problems would go away. However, although some of them did, I found that I had my own "money demons." I thought that once my worried, angry husband left, I could embark on a sensible financial path. But, at this point I came to the inescapable conclusion that there were historical events that had shaped my own bad habits. When I was a child, my parents were either very wealthy or almost destitute. We went from Venetian glass chandeliers specially made for our dining room to having to sell possessions to buy groceries. Since there was no margin or cushion when the bottom fell out, we would have to move. From the time I was born until I was married at the age of eighteen, we moved sixteen times. All of these moves were financially driven. There was a constant swing from one end of the spectrum where life was a party and spending was extravagant to the other end of the spectrum that was pure survival with no frills. When we had money there were absolutely no limits on what I could have or what I could do—*until the bottom fell out.* Because of this constant chaos, I developed very strong survival techniques. I learned to live without furniture, develop exciting potato recipes, and figure out how to survive at the age of seventeen with no money for groceries while my parents took an impromptu trip for two weeks.

On the other hand, I also knew how to spend money because my father taught me that spending was fun, and if you wanted something, you should have it immediately. When we had money we lived life on a grand scale. In addition to his spending, he gave large amounts of money away, including money that should have been earmarked for the future or the family. The picture I am trying to paint is that there was *no* plan for the future *at all* — there would always be another windfall to take care of everything.

Now in my fifties, I no longer had the structure of my marriage or the income to which I had become accustomed. During my marriage the income from my job was considered superfluous because my husband made so much more than I did. Also, it had been 24 years since I had been self-sufficient. On the plus side, my husband was no longer adding to the chaos. As I looked back on the past, I realized this was the first time I had total decision-making control over my life. I was on the threshold of a new life, and I knew I never again wanted to live with the system in which I had grown up or experienced in my marriage. I wanted a peaceful structure for my life — I had only one problem: I had no idea what one looked like. Although I had shed the chaotic lifestyle, I still had not developed the structure for financial peace. Even though I had studied many books on money, been involved in the stock market, and gone to investment seminars, my own personal financial life remained dark. It was at this point that my true money journey began.

Courtney's Story – Then

Three years ago I was convinced that I didn't have the money gene. I thought I had been given a bad genetic break similar to my total lack of a sense of direction. I had learned some compensating skills to get me around town, but I was not sure how to make up for my chaotic finances. I basically thought I just needed more money. Coupled with my belief in my unfortunate DNA was a firm belief that I would never be rich. Rich people lived on the same plane as beautiful blondes and women who carry small purses. In other words they were totally different from me. If I were ever to become rich, I believed I would need to change so radically that I might not be the same person. In my mind it was simply ordained that I would not be rich. I promptly married a man who became a minister to ensure my destiny.

Besides feeling lost when the subject turned to money, I also had a lot of fear surrounding money. I could not think of the future without seeing a picture of me as an old, broke, sick, homeless person. While I tried not to dwell on this image, it was firmly planted and could not be ignored. I was aware that I had no idea how to plan for my retirement, and whenever I would ask questions about it, I had no idea what the banker, broker, or financial planner was saying. It was as if they were speaking a different language—until they got to the numbers. "$300,000, or you will be destitute. $300,000 is the minimum. If you don't have $300,000..." POP!—The bag lady image would appear again.

I tried to talk to my husband about putting together a financial plan. Actually, what I really wanted was for him to just take over the finances, so I wouldn't have to deal with them. How I did this I'll never know, but I managed to marry a man who was even more afraid of money than I was. By default I had been chosen as our financial leader. I think we were both aware that our situation looked bleak.

I'm not through yet. I was fearful. I was ignorant. I felt incapable of understanding anything having to do with money, and I was also not sure I deserved money. As a child I had been taught not to be selfish. "Selfish" could mean a lot of different things. One of the things it meant was not being allowed to have something if everyone didn't have it. If I managed to get something, I was supposed to "share," which meant give it away. So I was not sure why I should spend energy trying to get money since I would probably have to give it away anyway. In fact, having money was almost like having a "kick me" sign taped to my back. If I had money in a savings account, I feared something bad would happen just so that I could pay for it out of my savings. That may not make sense to some people but that was what was programmed in my brain. If I had money, I feared other people would be upset with me because they didn't have money. If I had money, I would have to "deal with it," and I had no idea where to start.

I had incurred a certain amount of debt, and my efforts to pay it off were not working. Paying bills was so anxiety-producing for me that I had to force myself to sit down with the bills and deal with them. It was stressful in the extreme. I dreaded it as I would abdominal surgery. I never had enough money, and I would have to juggle every month. I was not sure why this was happening *every single month*. I understood the basic concept of budgeting, but it just never worked for me. I lived with a constant feeling of "not enoughness."

Any approach I made to the subject of money took great courage on my part. I was very fearful, and more often than not, I did not understand how money worked even after trying to find out. I was basically in the same isolated situation before and after asking questions. There were no people close to me that could help. I already told you about my husband. Suffice it to say, my immediate family and close friends were probably in the same boat I was. Looking back, I see that there were many times when the subject of money came up in my life, but since it was not a "polite" subject, the conversation was over before it could start. Money management is not taught in schools, nor is it taught in most families, so people are pretty much left to their own devices. How do you train yourself about money when you don't understand the books you're reading; when you don't understand the financial lingo; when the subject of money is taboo; and on top of all that, you're scared to death?

I realized I did have one person I could talk to about anything, and that was Lynn. Finally, here was an opening. In this way I was not as isolated as many people are because I had a friend—someone who wanted to learn about money with me.

It was while in counseling that I became aware that my problems with money were crippling me. As I resolved other issues, the money issue kept emerging. It became bigger and more worrisome. In other words, I could no longer look the other way. Money was the elephant in the living room.

When Lynn agreed to be my study partner, I finally had a way out of my financial maze. I did not know at that point that what I was really doing was setting out on a journey that would set me free.

~Chapter 2~
Lynn and Courtney's Story-Now

"When a man takes one step toward God, God takes more steps toward that man than there are sands in the worlds of time." -- The Work of the Christ

Lynn's Story – Now

At the time of this writing, I have moved from crisis management to money management. I no longer run out of money each month. I have savings accounts into which I make regular deposits. I am in the process of becoming debt-free. Even though I am still learning, I have financial peace. Working with my money on an everyday basis is pleasant, easy, and satisfying. Once a week I get cash from my bank account to cover the current expenses such as groceries, gas, personal items, and other needs. I pay my mortgage, utility, and miscellaneous bills as they come in—an abrupt change from the days of letting them stack up in a pile, hoping they'd go away.

Each morning I record my expenses for the previous day. When I first started tracking my expenses, I had planned to do it for a few months until I could get an idea of my outgo. Now, I find it so grounding that I cannot imagine living without tracking. It's an easy device for keeping me aware and in the moment. I really *enjoy* doing it! Handling my money in this manner makes me feel safe and in control of my finances. Even when there are financial challenges that I cannot meet immediately, tracking helps me look into the future and plan a solution to the problem. It takes care of my everyday finances with just a little effort on my part, and it enables me to focus most of my energy on setting up the structure for my financial future. Instead of being worried and fearful of the future, I now spend my energy planning and creating my new, exciting future.

There have also been other positive changes that have come about as a result of getting my money in order. In my previous money situation, I found it impossible to envision the future, much less plan for it. Working on a daily basis with the mechanics of money has given me a sense of continuity between the present and the future. I have a strong vision of what the future holds because I can see that I have more control over what happens to me. I know when I will be totally out of debt. I know what I will do with my money when I am out of debt. And I no longer feel I'm at the mercy of the unexpected. I know I can handle whatever comes.

In addition to having more peace about my finances, I simply have more peace, period. While I would possibly welcome expensive clothes, and a luxury car, I do not feel in the least that I *must* have these items or other items that previously symbolized wealth for me. While I enjoy the comforts and pleasures of the material world, I am not attached to them in the same way I was. I am content, and I am looking forward to what life brings.

Now that I am working with my money in the present, rather than spending future money, my money has become finite. This limitation has altered the value I place upon my money, my time, and my life. I do not waste. I understand my life is precious, and that my loved ones, friends, pets, money, and time are a gift to me. I am grateful for all of my blessings. There is another side to the blessing coin. While I embrace the gifts of life, I no longer tolerate chaotic, destructive, or wasteful things. I have cut out many activities that were not productive or enjoyable. I have even cut some that were enjoyable because I understand that there isn't time for everything. My life is much more balanced and centered.

Working with money has also changed the way I understand perfection and imperfection. I no longer strive for perfection. I embrace things as they are. I am more comfortable with imperfection. In the past, I would have insisted that my wardrobe be fashionable and expensive. In fact I would have done almost anything to achieve a perfect wardrobe. In other words, my wardrobe was an urgent concern for me. Now, while I am still aware of good taste, the urgency has gone. I can have what I want, but I don't place the same importance on those things. I make use of and enjoy things that money can buy. But I no longer feel the lack that drove me to try to get them at any cost.

I don't think I could have learned all these valuable lessons if I had not become conscious about what I was doing with money. Not only has my financial picture changed, but I am amazed at how much I have fundamentally changed as well. I will always be grateful for the joy that working with money has brought into my life. I look forward to a life that is tailor-made to fit me because I've let go of a grandiose illusion of a life I would have to try to occupy that is not really "me." I now know what the good life is.

Courtney's Story – Now

Although my financial picture has certainly changed, I have also made changes in my life that I didn't know would come about as a result of working with money. I am still learning about money, but I have come to a place of peace. I live in harmony with my money instead of living in constant fear. I enjoy paying my bills every month. I enjoy tracking my expenses. I enjoy filling out my income/expense record. I enjoy handling cash. I take an almost childlike enjoyment in all of these activities. I have started to enjoy spending money again without the underlying guilt and anxiety that always used to be part of shopping. Now it is a much clearer transaction because the enjoyment isn't clouded with worry.

My husband and I have increased our income, but this only happened after I started to organize our money differently. It happened as a result of my transformed relationship with money. My worry did not go away because more money came in. My worry started to go away and that attracted more money into my life.

One of the changes that is not so obviously connected to working with money is that my marriage is now more of a partnership. I began handling the finances and that took some of the pressure off of my husband. This enabled us to work together as a team as opposed to one person being completely in charge. The finances are still "my job," but I make sure my husband knows what is going on and that we're in agreement about our money. Going from our former approach to money to our present approach took a while and was *not* easy to say the least. Taking over the finances required me to give up the illusion of being taken care of. I decided money management was simply a task, and one of us needed to do it. This kind of clarity has made its way into other parts of my marriage and life, clearing out old patterns and obstacles and opening the way for exciting possibilities.

I no longer feel "there is not enough." I see abundance all around me, and I feel grateful most of the time. Like Lynn, my perception of the perfect/imperfect has altered. I accept things as they are more of the time. It is not necessary for everything to be "perfect" in order for me to feel safe. I appreciate things and people as they are and do not feel the urgent need to change them. I still wish to change things about my environment and relationships, but the uncomfortable urgency is gone.

While I am at peace about the way things are now, I am also excited about the future. I look forward to being able to expand my enjoyment of life and to contribute more to the lives of others. This is a surprising development considering I was afraid I would have to give money away. Now, giving money away is one of the most enjoyable parts of my life.

My understanding of friendship has changed. I have learned to be a more respectful and appreciative friend and to respect my own boundaries as well.

I have decided that far from being vulgar, scary, and untouchable, money is actually vital to my spiritual life. Working with money has changed my view of creation, how things operate in the universe, and who God is. I no longer believe that God does not want me to have money, or that God is not interested in money. I think that money is a starting place for us to learn about God and our relationship to the material world. Money may not be the ending point, but it is the arena in which we are tested. Working with money is definitely a central and necessary part of the spiritual life.

Working with money has opened the eyes of my true self. I am fascinated with the way money operates. I sometimes feel like I imagine Einstein must have felt when he studied light. Money is an integral part of the world, and it has led me to many wonderful discoveries—discoveries about God, about life, about relationships, and about myself. When I started studying money three years ago, I had hoped to get to the point where I had learned what I needed to know so I could go back to the "fun stuff" like art, cooking, reading, etc. To my amazement I have discovered that *money is fun*. I don't think I will ever get through learning about it. It is like an opening in space, leading me to galaxy after galaxy. When I began my money journey, I *thought* my destination was survival. I now know I will be on this incredible journey for the rest of my life. Who cares about the destination? It's the trip that is fun.

Using Money to Reshape Your Life

~Chapter 3~

Recognize that Your Present Money Behavior Is Not Working for You

"If the Angel deigns to come it will be because you have convinced her, not by tears, but by your humble resolve to be always beginning--to be a beginner."   Rainer Maria Rilke

It's possible to be an absolute genius at managing parts of your financial life, but if just one part of your money management system isn't working, the whole system will eventually be compromised.

As captain of your financial ship, you need to always be on the lookout for leaks or problems because even one tiny hole will eventually sink the entire ship. Unless you were raised by money geniuses, chances are that you've got a hole or two.

At this point in your quest for financial freedom, we will be looking for your weak points. While this may sound like as much fun as getting your teeth drilled, the benefits in all areas of your life will outweigh the pain.

Before I (CH) started studying money with Lynn, I was so afraid of money that I couldn't talk about it, read about it, or study it at all. So, you are way ahead of me because you bought this book! Believe me, no matter how bad it looks to you right now, there is hope for your finances. Here is a little quiz to help evaluate where you are so you can get to where you're going.

QUIZ

1. I feel _____ when I pay my bills each month.
    a. peaceful and grateful
    b. terrified and panic-stricken
    c. physically sick
    d. I have no feeling left
2. My spouse and I can talk about money
    a. with ease.
    b. if one of us is wearing a helmet.
    c. never.
    d. I didn't know I was supposed to talk about money with my spouse.
3. When I sit down and write out a spending plan, I feel
    a. in control of my money.
    b. imprisoned by my plan.
    c. instantly rebellious.
    d. What is a spending plan?
4. In relation to my friends, I feel like I know
    a. as much as they do.
    b. so much less than they do.
    c. I have no idea what they are talking about.
    d. I never talk about money with my friends.
5. When the subject turns to money, I am

a. embarrassed. Nice people aren't supposed to discuss money.
   b. interested. I am always looking to expand my knowledge.
   c. frightened. I immediately see myself living under a bridge, sucking down gruel through a straw.
   d. completely lost. What is a mutual fund?
6. Every month I save
   a. 10 percent.
   b. more than 10 percent.
   c. less than 10 percent.
   d. nothing. I don't make enough money to save anything, but when I get rich, I will start saving.
7. When I put money in savings, I feel
   a. happy because I am becoming financially independent.
   b. uneasy because there is money I am not supposed to spend.
   c. troubled because if I save money, something terrible will happen, and I'll have to take it out.
   d. I never put money in savings.
8. I pay for current expenses with
   a. cash.
   b. a check.
   c. a debit card.
   d. a credit card.
9. If I had to operate on a cash-only basis, I would feel
   a. in control of my money. Paying cash makes it very clear how much money I have.
   b. vulnerable. I could be robbed.
   c. less inclined to spend impulsively.

     d. afraid that I would run out of money.
10. When I spend money on myself, I feel
     a. grateful. I'm glad I can treat myself occasionally.
     b. nervous. I am not sure I am making the right decision when I buy something for myself.
     c. selfish. I am not supposed to spend money on myself.
     d. good for the moment, but anxious later on, because I just can't seem to say no to myself.
11. When I think about retirement, I feel
     a. secure. I am following a plan that will allow me to retire comfortably.
     b. petrified. I have no plan at all, and can barely pay my bills as it is.
     c. nervous. I have a plan, but it is inadequate. I'll fund it more when I get rich.
     d. doomed. I am too old to plan for retirement.
12. When I balance my checkbook, I am usually
     a. close to the bank balance.
     b. $50-$100 off.
     c. paying extra NSF charges.
     d. ...Are you supposed to balance your checkbook?

13. When I use my ATM or debit card, I
     a. always record the transaction *at that time.*
     b. record it later.
     c. sometimes forget to record it.
     d. ...You mean this money is coming out of my account?
14. At the present time, my debt load (not including my mortgage) is

a. nil.
b. 30 percent or more of my net income.
c. so heavy that I can only make the minimum payments and sometimes that is a stretch.
d. overwhelming. I can't even make my minimum payments.

Did you pinpoint any weak spots? You are not alone. The good news is that you are doing something to change your money situation. No matter how bad your money situation seems to be, there really is hope. Here are some common problems people have with money:

1. The belief that they must continue to support their children even when they are adults.
2. Emotional blocks to discussing money with their spouse.
3. Emotional blocks to even thinking about money.
4. Fear of having money.
5. Fear of not having money.
6. The belief that if they just had enough money, they wouldn't have to think about it or deal with it.
7. The belief that if they have a lot of money, they won't have time to have a life.
8. Many women believe if they have money, they won't have anyone to "take care of them."
9. No clue about what is going on in their checking account.

10. The belief that money is evil and will corrupt them.
11. The belief that if they have money, they have taken it away from someone else.
12. The belief that it's someone else's fault they don't have money.
13. The belief that they don't have enough money to manage.
14. The belief that they don't deserve to have money.

When you can recognize that what you are presently doing isn't working well for you, you have taken a very important step. The end of one thing is the beginning of another. You must truly be willing to end your old system and be willing to begin constructing a new one. It's not necessary at this point to know everything about your new system, but it is necessary to be willing to let go of your old one.

While you are making a transition from your old system to your new one, you will probably feel disoriented because you are learning new and unfamiliar skills. This period will not last too long, so be encouraged. You are on the right track.

~Chapter 4~
Make a Commitment to Educate Yourself about Money

"...the man who goes alone can start today; but he who travels with another must wait 'til that other is ready, and it may be a long time before they get off."— Henry David Thoreau

If you're like I (CH) was in the past, you spend a lot of time avoiding the subject of money because it is immensely worrisome to you. Here's what I did to overcome my *huge* emotional block—I got a partner who was almost as scared as I was about it, and together we forged ahead! If I had partnered up with a money expert, I probably would have decided there was no hope for me. Instead, I chose someone who had the same goal of learning about money. Even though our problems with money were different we could still work together. Here is what makes a partnership work well—you must both be committed to a schedule. Bet you thought I was going to say something a lot more profound, didn't you? But the truth is, what carried us through this process was our willingness to *show up and do the work*. (Julia Cameron explains this concept very well in her wonderful book, *The Artist's Way*.) Even when we were tired, or our schedules changed, or my spouse didn't support me, or we were discouraged and saw no benefits to continuing because things seemed like they were going backward, *we showed up, and we did the work.* It may seem silly to spend time educating yourself about money when you have so many urgent money issues. Your situation may seem to require a cataclysmic event such as winning the lottery, inheriting money, picking the right stock, etc., in order to cause a significant change, but the truth is very different from the appearance of your circumstances. What will really cause significant changes in your finances and in your life are *the small actions consistently taken.* Reading about money and discussing what you are learning with your partner is the very first action you need to take. Knowledge truly is power. Understanding money is worth the time it will take to educate yourself.

We talked to each other about the current book we were reading (see the appendix for our reading list) three mornings a week, and we did homework in between. If you're thinking, "But I don't have three mornings a week!" don't worry. We didn't either, and neither does anyone else we know. At one point, we got up at 5:30 a.m. so we could talk before Lynn left for her teaching job. We hope you won't have to resort to that hour, but the important point is to *show up and do the work!*

The reason we chose three times a week instead of once a week is that we needed to transform our thinking, and once a week just wasn't enough to do that. We needed more immersion and exposure to new ways of thinking to make the changes we needed to make—and you will too. Many times, the only thing that helped us read a chapter we *did not want to read* was the knowledge that we would have to talk with each other about it the next day. Most people call this accountability. We call it "scare yourself into doing something good." The point is, unless you have the determination of Arnold Schwarzenegger, you are not going to do this by yourself. Get a partner, and make a commitment.

Allow us to give you a word or two of advice about choosing your partner. Your partner needs to be trustworthy, safe, and motivated. If you feel that your partner might judge you or berate you, you will not be able to grow, and if your partner is not motivated enough to stick to the schedule he/she will drag you down as well. Although it may seem like your spouse is a good choice for a partner, because there are so many emotional issues at hand, it may be best to choose someone else. If there is no partner on the horizon, begin your own work and be alert for someone who wants to join you later.

It is time to start reading your first book. You can choose a book from our reading list or any financial book that interests you. We cannot overemphasize how important it is to do this reading and to do any exercises that may be required in the books you are reading. You will be reading these books in depth. Your goal is to immerse yourself in a new way of thinking. In order to do this kind of reading, you will probably read some passages several times; you will make notes on them, and you will discuss what you are reading with your partner. Of course you will be doing the recommended exercises in the books. You will turn over these new ideas in your mind. You will play with them; you will try them on for size, and you will suspend your current belief system long enough to be open to new ideas. You will plow through some material that may annoy you or with which you may not agree in order to learn something new. You will allow yourself some time to understand the things you are learning. You will not let yourself become frustrated because these new ideas don't make sense to you right away.

    The difference between reading for your own interest and reading for education is that education requires the student to be exposed to many different and often conflicting ideas. You may not entirely agree with some of the books you are reading. At some point in the future, you may reject some ideas and synthesize the rest, but do not reject too much information before you have had a chance to interact with it. Remember, you can always toss it out later. The object of this education is to expand your thinking. There are some books we highly recommend, but since everyone's path is different, you may read the books in any order you choose, and you may add or delete books. The book list provided contains the recommended reading list.

We began with *You Were Born Rich* by Bob Proctor. This book is about principles of prosperity and about *how* to incorporate right thinking into your plan of action. It is about your own potential to be wealthy.

Part of that process of changing your thinking may be uncomfortable. However, there will be other parts that will be lots of fun. Enjoy this process, and have fun with it. You are not in a race—you are on a journey. Don't forget to stop and have tea once in awhile. Hurrying will not get you there any faster.

Using Money to Reshape Your Life

~Chapter 5~

Now Do the Work

"The moment one definitely commits oneself, then, Providence moves too. Whatever you think you can do, or believe you can do, begin it. Action has magic, power, and grace." Goethe

    This is *the* critical step in your quest for financial freedom. Not every aspect of "doing the work" will be pleasurable. But, it will be worth it.

    Let us tell you the story of Bob. He worked for ten years to create the perfect garden complete with fountains, terraces, a pagoda, fragrant plants, a butterfly garden, woodland paths and climbing roses. Bob spent time in his garden almost every day. He can still remember the backbreaking labor it took to begin. Before he got to plant anything, he had to till his stubborn clay soil and amend it with heavy bags of peat moss. During this process his yard looked simply awful. It was basically tilled up dirt and rocks. He ran into tree roots that had to be moved, rocks that had to be taken out, and various other obstacles that had to be overcome, but Bob kept working. Soon he had the satisfaction of planting and watching his young plants grow. Although it was still hard work, he also began to enjoy and take great satisfaction from his labor. He had the setbacks of a winter freeze or a hot summer, but his progress continued to yield beautiful foliage. At the height of the garden's full beauty, his cousin came to visit. Bob proudly took him on a tour. "Wow!" said his cousin, "You are so lucky to get to live here. Isn't it amazing how beautiful God's creation is?"

"Yes, it is," said Bob rather indignantly, "But, you should have seen it when God was doing all the work by Himself."

Think of the most beautiful garden you have ever seen. It may look like a natural wonder, but we all know it just isn't so. Before the roses or the gently tinkling fountain and before the fragrant evergreen shrubs or the shade trees there was just dirt. Someone had to have the vision and make a plan, till the ground, plant the seeds, fertilize the plants, cover them in freezing weather, water them every day, prune them, etc. If the gardener stopped after he developed a plan, there would not be a garden. He had to go through the long and often tedious daily process of planting and tending the garden for it to become beautiful. Sometimes he will enjoy himself and commune with his garden and come away refreshed. Sometimes he will just be hot and tired. But, a good gardener knows that plants need attention in order to flourish. Your financial life may look like a patch of dirt right now, but the combination of doing the work while holding the vision will produce a lifestyle more pleasing than the beautiful garden we just described.

You can be financially independent and as wealthy as you want to be, but it means paying the price like Bob did for his beautiful garden. The good news is you don't have to dig in the dirt forever—just commit a certain amount of time every day, and your life will be transformed. When you consider the alternative of struggling with money for the rest of your life, your choice becomes much easier. In the past you didn't know how to drive a car. Now you may drive every day with ease. At one point in time, you may have become winded from doing 10 crunches; now you do 30 with ease. What we are trying to say is that while you may choose to do something that requires a lot of effort on your part, there will come a day when it is easy, and you are very glad you made the choice you did.

Here are some helpful strategies and reminders for pushing through and handling the stress that will accompany this transition.

1. Do not get discouraged if you figure out that changing your money management behavior will take longer than you first anticipated. Just be determined to take it a step at a time. As you begin to clear the clutter from your money closet, it is going to get more disorganized than you can imagine before order is restored. Besides the things that are piled on the floor, you will find other things cropping up and begging for attention that you had completely forgotten

about. We would tell you not to be surprised, but you will be anyway. This is not a linear process—you are making a lifestyle change from chaos into order. If you keep working the plan, you will emerge from chaos into a peaceful, balanced life. At this point, working the plan means educating yourself about money and doing the exercises in the books you are reading. I (CH) had started really making an effort to save money on groceries. I had read in *The Tightwad Gazette* about bulk buying and visiting different grocery stores for their advertised sale items. Changing over to this method of purchasing groceries took a lot of time and energy in the beginning—now it is easy. But one day I came home after driving to several grocery stores and was so proud of myself for saving five dollars. My husband met me at the door to tell me he had overdrawn his checking account by *four hundred dollars*. Suddenly, my five dollars hardly seemed worth celebrating. Expect things to happen that make you want to give up. Be prepared to pick yourself up and start again. When you plant a seed in the ground, for a long time it looks like nothing is happening. But in reality, that seed is growing, and at some point in the future, the plant pushes through the earth and becomes visible. It is the same way with the work you are doing now. It may seem frustrating

because you don't see the changes as fast as you would like. These changes are happening. There is always a period of time during which gestation is taking place. Be patient. Your changes are worth waiting for.
2. Realize that each positive act will bring a positive result—however the results may not be immediate or even foreseeable. You may need to accept by faith that positive acts, however small, are cumulative. I (LB) realized that not ordering iced tea when I went out to eat would mean extra money. In three months I easily saved $37 from that one small decision. I simply made choices about the money *I already had.* I rerouted my money to build financial strength simply by making small, easy choices whenever I could. I felt no deprivation from saving the money. Iced tea was not that important to me, so I didn't miss it. Instead of feeling deprived, I felt empowered each time I made a deposit. The point is to start with a small, obtainable step and add steps as your confidence grows. *Please be aware that each act, whether positive or negative, charts a course into the future. Choose your actions with care. It is exactly these small, seemingly insignificant steps that build wealth.*

3. Don't rush through the books. Take time to interact with them. If something interests you, chew on that awhile. Study and learn. *Acquire* this knowledge — don't just read it and forget it. We have read some books three times *thoroughly* because each reading was beneficial. Understand that the point is not to see how many books you can read. The point is to change the way you think about and respond to money. Changing habits takes time and effort, but the changes will bring enormous results.
4. Don't beat yourself up for not changing as quickly as you expect to. Changes take time. Change is a process that cannot be rushed or forced. Each attempt to change brings you closer to your goal and makes every subsequent attempt easier.
5. Be protective of yourself. While you are making changes, do not expect your friends or family members to understand and support what you are trying to do. Later on, when you are on solid ground, you may share with whomever you wish.
6. Many people want to prematurely engage their spouse in this process. It is generally best to start the process and allow your spouse time to see the positive changes that are happening. Think about this — requiring your spouse to instantly change because *you* have decided to make changes is not only impractical, it is not being respectful of your spouse's ability to make his or her own choices.

This may sound exclusionary, but all positive financial changes you make that help you eventually help your spouse and your marriage.

7. Learn to live with the anxiety of change because no real change happens without it. Even good change can be painful, difficult, or slow. Your anxiety doesn't mean you are doing something wrong. It is part of every creative process. Make friends with it! Anxiety is the driving force that causes change.

8. Make small changes. These are very significant. Here are some examples: clean out your closet, and get enough sleep instead of watching television. Like we said before, changing your money behavior is going to change the rest of your life. You may decide to clear out some clutter from your life—for example, people who want to talk on the phone, and who distract you from what you should be doing; people who are negative or critical; friendships that require too much maintenance for little or no return; unnecessary meetings, shopping, or over-scheduling. Only you know what is cluttering your life. Now—how do you get rid of it? Just a suggestion—don't unnecessarily alienate people with whom you will no longer be spending time. Simply get busy with your new life. It is not that you don't *want* to go to the ballgame or to lunch, it is just that you don't

have time. It will surprise you how quickly your friends will forget to call you, and the added benefit of this method is that nobody gets hurt. It is not always necessary to confront people. You do not need anybody's permission to do what you are responsible for doing.
9. Be persistent. Real life requires diligence and work. The good news is that you will enjoy the benefits of your efforts for the rest of your life.

Be kind to yourself. You may feel disoriented and moody during this time of change. Do your best, but don't expect perfect behavior from yourself right now. Try to do things that will alleviate some of your stress such as making sure you get enough sleep, eating well, exercising, and having quiet time for yourself. It may be necessary to cut other things out of your schedule in order to take care of yourself.

Your positive changes will definitely bring their own rewards. But sometimes an immediate reward is in order. Do whatever you have to do to get yourself to take action—including bribing yourself. When we are faced with doing something we would rather not do, we tell ourselves that if we roll up our sleeves and do this task, we can have a special treat, such as reading for an hour, going to the movies, hot fudge sundaes—you get the idea.

~Chapter 6~

Now Begin Applying Your Knowledge to Your Own Finances

"I'd gone through life believing in the strength and competence of others; never in my own. Now, dazzled, I discovered that my capacities were real. It was like finding a fortune in the lining of an old coat." -- Joan Mills

When you apply the strategies outlined in this chapter to your finances, you will also be making other life changes. If you didn't realize it before now, you will understand that finances affect every part of your life. As you get your money in order, you will find your life coming into balance. At this point you will begin using a new organizational structure for income and expenses. We call this "Getting Current." The six strategies in "Getting Current" will give you control over your money.

Getting Current

1. Begin to work with cash for current expenses.

The reason you want to start using cash is because it helps you pay attention to spending money in a

Using Money to Reshape Your Life

different way than check registers or credit card statements. The use of cash triggers part of your brain that checks and credit cards do not. Using cash is not the same thing as putting yourself on a budget. Using cash will simply make you more aware of the value you get each time you spend money. It will help you get more of what you like or want and less of what you don't like or want. Let's say you would like a beautiful wool winter coat. The one you really like costs more money than you have ever spent on one piece of clothing before. You can either spend the necessary amount and get the coat you want, or you can attempt to satisfy yourself with a less expensive coat. What often happens when you choose the less expensive item is that you are not satisfied. You may buy several less expensive coats—and spend more money—than if you had just gotten what you wanted in the first place. This same phenomenon often happens on a diet. Sometime during the diet you may get a craving for chocolate. Chocolate is not on your diet, so in a futile attempt to satisfy yourself, you raid the refrigerator and eat various approved foods and then eat the chocolate anyway! It would have been better to have a Hershey's Kiss and be happy in the first place. Using cash will help you to know what you really want and to make more satisfying purchases. Many people hesitate to use cash because they are afraid they will feel deprived. In reality, the opposite occurs. Paying cash will help you understand what will satisfy you and what is simply junk-buying.

If you need help working with cash, try the envelope system. Here's how it works. First, label an envelope for each category of current expenses—every person's categories will vary. Here is what I (CH) started with: groceries, eating out/entertainment, haircuts, housing supplies, gas, clothes and personal items. At regular intervals put as much cash as you think you will need for that time period in each envelope. There is no right or wrong amount. Your goal is to have the cash last you until the next time you go to the bank. You will probably find that it will take several months for your projected amount to align with your actual amount. You will also move cash from one envelope to another. This is fine. By moving cash from one category to another, you are training yourself to understand that each choice has a cost. If you save in one area, you can spend in another. After several months you may want to add another envelope. We call it the "BYOB" fund (Be Your Own Bank). You will see that if you save five dollars you can funnel this into your BYOB envelope—this envelope will eventually become your cash reserve fund. (More on this in a later chapter.)

You will be training yourself to understand a very critical concept—*every dollar counts*. In fact, *every penny counts*. Following are some things that might happen.

You will discover you are buying something for which you do not have a category. For me (CH) it was thread. Is that housing? Is it hobbies? Clothes? The point is that before I started using the envelopes, part of my brain believed that money spent on sewing notions *didn't count*. You would be surprised how much money you can spend on things that "don't count"! What are you not counting? Batteries? Photo supplies? Magazines? Your favorite coffee shop? The point of using cash is not to develop a budget immediately. First, Choices about money are neither right nor wrong, but knowing where your money goes helps you decide how important each purchase is to you.

2. Begin to track your income and expenses.

Track every purchase including cokes, stamps, toll charges, etc., and all income as well. Tracking means writing down the date, the amount spent, and what was purchased. Example:

1/22/02	Breakfast	$6.81
1/24/02	Coke	$ .50
1/25/02	Gas	$9.57

You will need a small portable notebook. It is better to track your purchase at the time of purchase.

So carry this notebook with you everywhere. If you are married, your spouse may or may not be cooperative in your new venture. See if your spouse will at least agree to save receipts and deposit them in a pre-determined location for you to enter into your notebook. When I (CH) first started, my husband put receipts by the phone for me to pick up and track.

Tracking is an integral part of the system. *Do not attempt to leave it out.* This may be the most important exercise you do. We plan to track for the rest of our lives, and we hope you will too. While tracking has long-term rewards, you will start to see the benefits of tracking almost immediately. Tracking produces a higher awareness level; it makes a note of all energy that leaves and all energy that comes in. Understand that your tracking is not an exercise in valuation; it is an exercise in observation and awareness. Here are some things that may happen. You will require a balance in many areas of your life, including relationships. For instance, you may have a high maintenance person who doesn't add much to your life. You may become resentful that you are giving because this person requires attention, not because you are choosing to be a blessing. Tracking lets you know that you require balance. You may find yourself organizing your schedule and environment differently. You will become more aware of the disparity in prices of similar items. You will become more conscious of what you spend. Tracking signals your brain that you are making changes. It is a *catalyst* that puts you in alignment with a different money flow.

3. **At the end of each month fill out an income/expense record.**

Income is any money that comes in from any source, such as salary, child support or gifts. An expense is any money that goes out. Your categories and your income/expense record will be different from anyone else's. Everyone has his or her own unique categories. Start with basic categories, and as you continue this process you will add, subtract, and change categories. The important thing is to have specific well-defined categories without having so many that they become overwhelming. For example, do not include batteries, laundry detergent, shower gel, or dog toys in your grocery category. You want to know what you are spending on food for that category. The other categories such as personal care, household goods, pet items, and anything else you can buy at the supermarket each have their own categories. Your goal is to get a yearly amount for each category. This will help you change from a monthly to a yearly orientation. Your expenses include many items that are not monthly expenses such as wedding gifts, Christmas, auto registration, fishing and hunting licenses, vacation expenses, insurance if you pay annually or quarterly, housing maintenance, tires—you get the idea. The only way you will know what your total yearly expenses are is to track your expenses over a period of one year. Once you have an idea about how much you spend annually for food/clothing/housing, you will have more control over your finances. It is important to move from living on a monthly basis to a yearly basis and to a *total cost basis*. For example you need to know the total amount your house is going to cost—not just the mortgage payment. You may have to take it on faith that this income/expense record exercise will be very beneficial. You will see the benefits for yourself after tracking over a period of time and filling out the monthly income/expense record. This exercise is an integral part of the process of taking control of your life.

Using Money to Reshape Your Life

Monthly Tracking Sheet	Date
Income	
Salary	
Royalties	
Child Support	
Alimony	
Other Income	
Total Monthly Income	
Expenses	
Mortgage	
Extra Principal	
Phone	
Cell Phone	
Internet	
Electricity	
Gas	
Water	
Health Insurance	
Auto Insurance	
Homeowners Insurance	
Groceries	
Eating Out	
Pet Expenses	
Medical Expenses	
Prescriptions	
Car Payment	

Auto Expenses	
Gifts	
Clothes	
Personal Items	
Entertainment	
Books, Newspapers	
Travel Expenses	
Charitable Donations	
Total Monthly Expense	
Savings	
Annual Income Acct.	
Investment Acct.	
Financial Independence Act	
Spending Acct.	
Debt Freedom Acct.	
Total Monthly Savings	

4. Enact the law of reciprocity.

The law of reciprocity is a universal law that says what you give you will get back; what you sow you will reap; what goes around comes around. We are assuming you would like more money. The quickest way to get more money is to give more money. *We realize this might sound absurd, but we wouldn't say it if it didn't work.* The standard amount is ten percent. Why ten percent? We cannot claim to know the answer to that, but most of the world religions for all of recorded history have chosen ten percent as the amount to give. If you are like most people, in order to give ten percent you will have to step out in faith. In other words, you may not be able to work this out on paper—you may just have to do it. This advice may seem to run counter to sound financial practice. However, because this type of giving invokes the law of reciprocity, it always "works."

When you give, you also prepare yourself to receive.

- Giving ten percent on a regular basis helps you understand that you are a steward. When you understand you are a steward, you know you are not operating alone.
- Giving ten percent helps you understand that you are in charge of the remaining ninety percent. This may seem obvious, but many people do not feel ownership of their money. This is one reason why they overspend—to get rid of it as fast as possible. They simply do not believe they deserve it.
- Giving ten percent helps you understand that money is not your source. From this point on, it becomes easier to observe how money operates.
- Giving ten percent takes the fear out of dealing with money. Before giving ten percent, it seems like there

is not enough money. But after giving a tenth, the sense of lack is gone. It is replaced by a sense of being a part of a much larger whole in which all things work together.
- Giving ten percent helps you know that your money is important and makes a difference. You don't have to "get rich" before you can start helping people.
- Giving ten percent helps you manage your money better.

"But," you say, "I'm in debt. I'm poor. I say no to my own children more than I want to." What you *must* understand is that money is dynamic. The amount of money you have right now is not stagnant—your current income can change. Not having enough is a thought you *must not* support or dwell upon. It is only a circumstance, and circumstances change. The thing that makes them change the fastest is giving ten percent. If you wait for things to change *before* you give ten percent, you may be waiting a long time. Do the right thing *now*.

5. Stop using credit cards, debit cards and ATM cards.

There is a part of your brain that thinks you are getting something for nothing when you use anything but cash. You will become much more aware of spending money at the *time of purchase.* We do not feel it is necessary for you to rid yourself of all credit cards. They serve a purpose. They may be necessary at times—for instance when renting a car, booking hotel reservations, etc.

6. **Make a debt repayment schedule.**

    We have listed this last for a reason. After you learn to predict and manage your current expenses, you have a much better idea of how much money you can commit to debt repayment. Make a list of all your debts. Note the balance and monthly payment. Then list your debts in order starting with the lowest balance. Total all of your balances, and all of your monthly payments. Now you know how much you are spending every month on debt and how much debt you have. At this point, try to add money to the debt payment with the lowest balance. Do not add an unreasonable amount because you will not be able to sustain your plan, and we don't want you to become frustrated. Think of this as a marathon, not a sprint.

DEBT REPAYMENT SCHEDULE

Debt Name	Current Balance	Minimum Pay-off	Debt Pay-off Accelerator $100	Months to Pay-off	Months to Pay-off w/o Accelerator
Visa	$972,00	$24.00	$124.00	8 months	41 months
MasterCard	$2,755.00	$55.00	$179.00	15 months	50 months
Discover	$4,300.00	$86.00	$265.00	16 months	50 months
Car 1	$8,150.00	$359.00	$624.00	13 months	23 months
Car 2	$11,650.00	$308.00	$932.00	13 months	38 months
Mortgage	$94,076.00	$604.00	$1536.00	61 months	324 months
Total	$121,903.00	$1,436.00	$1,536.00	126 Mo.	
Years to total debt freedom			→	10.5 years	27 years

When you pay off your first debt, take that monthly payment and add it to the second debt on the list. This is where you will start to see some definite progress. When that debt is paid, take that monthly payment plus the first debt's monthly payment and add it to the third debt on the list. Your total monthly payment remains the same. In the chart above, the accelerator amount is $100.00. This amount is added to the debt with the lowest balance—in this case Visa—to make the payment $124.00. The rest of the debts are being maintained with just the minimum balance. The idea is to pay off the top debt and then roll the payment down to the next debt and eliminate the second debt. If we took the $100.00 accelerator and divided it among all the debts, it would not have the power to accomplish the same thing. It is important to focus the accelerator amount rather than diffuse it. It is equally important to pay the same total amount until all the debts are paid in full. In other words, when Visa is paid, off use the $24.00 you were paying to Visa and apply it to the next debt.

You will notice we have not included interest rates in our chart. If you are doing the roll down system of debt payment, the interest rate is not as important as you might think because the debts will be paid off quickly. The interest rate may make only a slight difference in the number of months to pay off the debt. If it is your intention to maintain a debt, the interest rate becomes important. However, since you will be paying the debt off quickly, the interest rate will not have as much time to accrue.

Here's another idea: If you have money left over in your cash envelopes, funnel that money into another envelope labeled "debt repayment" and use it to accelerate your payments. Committing to a certain amount each month doesn't mean you can't add more when possible. Add this amount to the debt at the top of the list. For more information on this system of debt repayment, read the book, *Conscious Prosperity*, by John Moore.

It is important to do each part of the system. At first, most people shy away from working with cash. You may not see the harm in using your ATM card. You may not feel it necessary to track every purchase. *Please remember your previous money system did not work well for you. There is a reason it didn't. This system will retrain your brain about money and encourage your money to grow.*

Using Money to Reshape Your Life

~Chapter 7~
Goal Setting for the Future

"Thou shalt decree a thing, and it shall be established unto thee: and the light shall shine upon thy ways." -- Job 22:28

Before you set goals for your future, you have to know what kind of future you want. This may sound elementary, but thinking of your own future can be a very difficult thing to do. It was for both of us. I (CH) unwittingly ended up dwelling on the bag-lady image I had of myself. I didn't want to spend a whole lot of time on *that* vision, but I didn't know what to replace it with. I (LB) had trouble imagining myself as a financially independent person without a financially successful husband. After the divorce my picture of the future had changed. Both Courtney and I worried about how all of this change was going to happen. It was hard to believe we could have a future. Perhaps this was because we were carrying the debts from our past, and we just couldn't imagine life after debt.

The future is difficult to contemplate while you are still in debt. Debt ties you to the past. First, you must settle your debts. Don't be concerned if this takes some time. Then, you must interact with the present. In order to see your future as you want it to be you must learn how to affect your environment in the present. Using your time and money wisely in the present will give you a foundation on which to build your future vision and your future relationship with money. This is what tracking your money helps you do. It grounds you in the present and gives you the raw material with which to build your future.

Whatever your dreams for the future are, your *goal* must be to develop financial peace. It doesn't matter if you are 22 or 59—you can achieve this!

What is financial peace? Well, it's not just having a lot of money although it might include wealth. It is being able to create and maintain a life full of joy, purpose, peace, meaning, health, harmony, and of benefit to all who come in contact with you. When you have financial peace, you will cease to struggle with money or be afraid of it. You will know what money can do and what it cannot do. You will be able to use money as a tool to make your life better. You will know that you have power over money—it does not have power over you.

Once you get a picture of what you want your future to be, you have a direction. You have a purpose. Dwell on that picture. One way to help you develop your own picture is to create a vision board. Do this by making a collage using magazines and poster board. Just cut out any pictures that speak to you about what you want in your own life. Be sure to place your vision board where you can see it often. And while you're dwelling on that wonderful picture, we have some tools in the next chapter we'd like to share with you to help you take action right now. *The combination of future vision and present action, even if they seem worlds apart, is a very powerful combination.*

Using Money to Reshape Your Life

~Chapter 8~

Taking It to the Next Level—
Saving, Investing, Spending

"There's no use trying," Alice said: "One can't believe impossible things." "I daresay you haven't had much practice," said the Queen. "When I was your age, I always did it for half-an-hour a day. Why, sometimes I've believed as many as six impossible things before breakfast." -- Lewis Carroll

Continue using all six strategies outlined in Chapter Six. They are:

1) Work with cash for current expenses.
2) Track your income and expenses.
3) Fill out monthly income/expense records.
4) Enact the law of reciprocity.
5) Stop using credit/debit cards and ATM cards.
6) Make a debt repayment schedule.

You are about to solve a lot of your money problems. You may not even know what your money problems are—other than not having enough. We hope you are aware by now that we are interested in your money system, and that having a structure is key. If something is wrong with your system, lots of money is not going to solve that problem. We see people every day who have lots of money, but their financial lives are completely out of control. As a result, other areas of their lives, work, and/or relationships are also a complete disaster.

The following tools will provide a structure for your money and will also help to transform your relationship with money. Before you read about the five accounts, let us encourage you not to become frustrated. This chapter presents a lot of detailed and new information that may not make sense at first. You may need to read this chapter several times. As you interact with these accounts, things will become clearer to you. Don't get discouraged. As you take action, your understanding will grow.

The Five Accounts

As much as we would like to, we cannot claim credit for the five accounts. You can find them in the book, *Money Is My Friend* by Phil Laut and in the Fredric Lehrman tapes, *Prosperity Consciousness*. Briefly, opening five accounts while you have very little money may seem ridiculous, but this is exactly the time to open them. The five accounts are storehouses for your money. Remember the famous line in the movie, *Field of Dreams*: "If you build it, they will come." In other words *do not wait* to get money in order to start treating your money seriously. Start with whatever you have. There are several purposes for using the five-account system:

1. To retrain your brain about money.
2. To teach you about the functions of money.
3. To change your behavior regarding money.
4. To give money that is coming to you a place to live.
5. To attract more money into your life.

Think of your financial system as a car and money as the gas that fuels your car. If your transmission is not working, putting more gas in the tank won't solve the problem. The problem is with the transmission. That needs to be repaired, and unless it is, no amount of gas will make any difference. When your car is running smoothly, then the gas "makes it go." Money only helps you do what you are already doing. Money by itself does not change the system.

"Okay," you say, "I've got it, but I still don't know what is wrong with my system. How can I fix it when I don't know what is wrong?" The good news is you don't have to know what is wrong at this point. *If you follow the rules of the five accounts, the five accounts will almost fix your problems for you.* You don't have to have any idea how or even why this works before you start to benefit from the five accounts. The problems you have will solve themselves as you begin to put the system into operation. We will go over some of the reasons why they do work, but if it still doesn't make any sense to you, it doesn't matter. It will start to work after you start to work with the accounts.

You can open five savings accounts at the bank to get started. After you work with the accounts and get the hang of it, you can move them to other higher interest bearing accounts at your own discretion.

The Income Account

This account is the intake and holding account. The rule for this account is that all money coming into your life must be deposited into the Income Account before it goes anywhere else. Even if all your money is designated for bills, do not put your paycheck into your checking account. Put it first into the Income Account. One benefit of this account is that it will provide you with a record of all the money you earn each year. But, that is just a benefit — it isn't the reason you have established this account. Obviously, you will be transferring money from your Income Account into your other accounts. However, it is unlikely you will transfer *all* the money out of this account. So the money will accumulate over time and provide a money cushion.

For some reason all the money deposited into a checking account gets spent. But if it is in a savings account from which money is transferred to cover your checks, some of the money actually stays put. J. P. Morgan said, "Fortunes are made and lost with small money." People in the financial industry call these small amounts of money "breakage," and huge fortunes are made simply from breakage. This is the account into which all income goes, and from which money is transferred into all the other accounts.

The Financial Independence Account

The Financial Independence Account is the account that is the foundation for your entire money system. The long-term purpose of this account is to build the permanent wealth that will eventually make you financially independent! You will be able to live off of the interest generated by the principal sum. The one rule for this account is that any money going in can never be withdrawn. Fortunately, we are not there to see the look on your face or hear your gasps! Nevertheless, that is the rule for this account.

You can begin this account with the money you saved in your BYOB (Be Your Own Bank) envelope. (See chapter 6 to review the envelope system.) If you don't have a BYOB envelope, just begin with any amount. You will be able to take out the interest earned by this account at periodic intervals and experience spending money that your money has earned for you. This experience will mentally prepare you for financial independence. Make a big production of spending the interest. For example, a friend of mine and I (LB) used the interest from the Financial Independence Account to go to an elegant restaurant for a leisurely lunch. We ordered what we wanted without any concern for the prices on the menu. At the end of the meal we had spent close to $100, and there was still money left to put back into the account. For close to $100, both my friend and I got to feel like a million bucks. With each financial independence experience, the brain becomes more able to fully receive financial independence. The experience of spending money that your money produced allows you to practice for your future as a financially independent person.

Another benefit of this account is that as your balance grows, you will break through your unconscious money ceiling, which most of us have. If you can't manage to get more than $1,000 in your savings account before something happens, and you need to take money out, your unconscious ceiling is $1,000. Your unconscious tells you that you don't want to go above that amount.

Because you cannot withdraw the money, and you continue to make regular deposits, your balance will break through your ceiling. Once you are able to break through, you will be amazed how much easier it is to attract more money. You may think this sounds impossible, but remember what we said when it starts happening. You heard it here first!

The Annual Income Account

The purpose of this account is to build cash reserves equal to one year's living expenses. Yes! You will be able to live for one year without ever going to work. Here are the rules for this account: Decide on the amount necessary for you to live for one year. Divide this number by 365 days to get how much you will need each day. This exercise breaks down the big number into smaller numbers that your unconscious brain can absorb and understand. After you decide how much you need, tell your unconscious to go out and get the daily amount, and see what happens. Example: $36,500 divided by 365 days = $100 a day. While you are telling your unconscious to go out and get $100 a day to put into this account, make deposits of any amount just to get started. Don't get discouraged if your unconscious is slow on the uptake!

The other purpose of this account is to free yourself from thinking you are so dependent on your job. Feeling more independent can stimulate your creative juices and help you discover fun ways of increasing your income.

The Spending Account

This account will help you have a balanced money system. We all have had mixed messages about spending money. On one hand, most people will readily admit it's fun to spend money, but on the other hand, what about saving? If we spend money on something we want, has it been wasted? We're not completely sure. Should we have saved it for a "rainy day"? Therefore, the rule for this account is that you *must* spend all the money in this account. Keep only enough in it for the account to stay open.

The act of having to spend all the money in this account can help you stop your impulse spending. This account will also help make you aware of what you *really* want and give you permission to have it.

Here is the fun part. Think about what you want. This account allows you to spend money on what you really want—not on what you think you should want. And, it removes guilt associated with spending money on yourself because the rule is you have to spend all the money. When was the last time you've heard a rule like that? One of the things that causes overspending is not being honest about what we want.

There are a couple of ways to use the Spending Account. Whenever your Spending Account gets to a certain balance, you spend the money, or you spend it at regular intervals regardless of the balance. This account teaches you to receive money and to celebrate the things money can buy. One last thing—don't buy boring necessary items like prunes or paper towels with this money. Spending this money should include fun and excitement, so spend it on stuff you want with the enthusiasm you had as a kid. And, this time there will be no one to disapprove—not even you!

The Investment Account

The purpose of this account is to create more money. As money is earned in this account, it is reinvested. Eventually the gains from this account will fund your permanent wealth (Financial Independence Account), your current spending (Spending Account), and cash reserves (Annual Income Account).

The Investment Account may seem just like the Financial Independence Account, but in the Financial Independence Account you never touch the principal. In the Investment Account, you are constantly touching the principal and taking sufficient risks to grow your money.

Okay, you may be wondering how much to put into each account. A good rule of thumb is 10 percent of your monthly income—which you will divide however you wish among the five accounts. If you can save more than 10 percent, that's great. As you work with these principles, you will be able to save more.

Another question you may have is "What is the difference between the Financial Independence Account, Annual Income Account, and Investment Account?" At first, these all seem to be the same thing. But they are all addressing different functions of money.

The Financial Independence Account retrains your brain to think of yourself as a soon-to-be financially independent person. You may change from thinking of yourself as just an employed person who is always going to be dependent on wages to thinking of yourself as someone who has the ability to become financially independent.

The Annual Income Account retrains your brain to stop being at the mercy of events and circumstances. When you have saved an amount equal to a year's worth of expenses, you will be practically impervious to anything that might happen. This account takes much of the fear and anxiety out of the picture. In its place it brings power and strength.

The Investment Account retrains your brain to create wealth. You will change from a person hoping your employer will give you a raise to a person who thinks creatively about how to generate money. Ideas about how to make money will begin to come to you as never before.

The Spending Account trains you to spend money without guilt or excess. One of the functions of money is as a medium of exchange. You may already think you know how to spend money, but interacting with the Spending Account will train you to negotiate for what you really want. You will stop spending unconsciously or excessively because your spending will become *intentional.* You will understand that you are in charge of your money—that you have more choices than you thought you did. The Financial Independence Account amasses *permanent wealth.* The Annual Income Account provides *cash reserves.* The Investment Account *creates more money* with which to fund your other accounts. These three functions are each necessary for the development of a sound financial base. The purpose of these accounts is not just to collect money in savings, but also to *create a structure for wealth!*

You may also be wondering if each account is really necessary, or if you could get by on fewer accounts or even just on a savings account and a checking account. At first the five accounts may seem too complicated. But what happens is that the five accounts *organize* your money, and free your brain for more creative endeavors. The five accounts almost do the work for you. Your job is to open the accounts and to systematically fund them. The amount of money you put into each account is not as important as the discipline of following the system and retraining your brain about money. The more your understanding grows, the more money you will have to put into your accounts. First, you make the commitment and *begin* the discipline. Then, the money comes to you. *Do not say to yourself,* "When I get the money, then I will open the accounts." Open them now.

You may be wondering how to use your checkbook in conjunction with the five accounts. What you need to do is limit the use of your checking account. If you are like most people, you use your checking account for current expenses, and you may not balance your checkbook every month. You think this system provides you with instant tracking, but all you really know is that you spent $83 at the grocery store. Was it all for groceries, or did you rent a video and develop film as well? It will be that much easier to balance your checkbook because the number of checks written will be greatly reduced.

Your checking account may also give you a false sense of having a cushion. If you are like us, you used future money to pay for present expenses, and somehow never got through paying for the past. *Using cash for current expenses separates your past from your present.* This is an important concept for your brain to understand. *Use your checkbook to pay bills and debt payments only.* Examples are your utility bills, your mortgage, your credit card payments, and your insurance payments. Maintain the minimum balance your bank requires to keep the account open. Do not put any extra money in your checking account. After writing out your bills, transfer just the necessary amount from your income account into your checking account to cover them.

One benefit of this system is that you will not go into a store thinking you have money in your checking account. If you find something and decide to purchase it, have the store hold it for you while you get the cash from your Spending Account. (This item would be something you had not included in current expenses.) You may think this will cause you an awful lot of trouble. That's the point! You are consciously retraining your brain. This process will make you more acutely aware of impulse spending. Remember, if your present money management system worked well for you, you would not be reading this book. This process gives you a chance to decide if you really want the item.

The five accounts are very systematic, visible, and measurable. They are designed to organize your money.

However, the five accounts do not function in a vacuum. As you introduce these five accounts into the rest of your life, there will most likely be some changes in other areas of your life. Your life is an organic system. Change a part, and the whole must accommodate those changes.

Rewiring your brain is like moving into a new house. You don't wake up one day in your new house with everything put away and the pictures hung. You see the new house, and you can't wait to live there, but there are things you have to do. You have to pack. You have to live in your old house surrounded by boxes. Your dog may even decide to get sick on moving day. Your children will whine. Dust balls will accumulate. Making coffee becomes a gargantuan task because you don't know where the coffee's packed. After moving everything into your new house, you are exhausted. You really want to get comfortable and take a couple of days off, but you have to clean. You have to unpack. You have to decide where everything is going to go. You may have to get rid of some things you thought you could use in your new house. You may need to acquire new things you didn't need in your old house. You may feel disoriented in your new house for a while. You can't remember exactly where you put stuff. But after living there for a few weeks, you become acclimated. And after a few months, you start to feel at home. Changing yourself—especially regarding money—is a lot like moving into a new house. It's not easy, but it is worth it.

The five accounts are designed to move you into financial independence. It is at this point that you may encounter resistance from your family, friends, or even yourself. What happens is that as you change your financial awareness and behavior, you change.

Give yourself permission to disturb the status quo of your system. This will naturally impact other people. There are certainly times that are appropriate for working on changing relationships, but that is not the focus of our book. In our experience, working on your own stuff before you work on relationships with others works best. If you attempt to work on relationships first, perhaps to set up a support system for your own personal changes, you will be wasting energy and become distracted from your goal.

Do your own stuff first! By making your own positive changes, you will ultimately be helping those with whom you come in contact.

There will be a time during which you will have detached yourself from expensive and unsatisfying activities that used to keep you connected to friends. As you let go of some of the activities that are no longer financially viable or personally satisfying, you may find yourself a little bit lonely or at loose ends. This is normal. The positive benefits of all your work will be more than worth the discomfort you feel at this point. This is a temporary condition, and in time you will find yourself enjoying people and activities that enrich your life.

~Chapter 9~
Beyond Financial Independence

"It's a funny thing about life; if you refuse to accept anything but the best, you very often get it." -- Somerset Maugham

If you have been working with the strategies in Getting Current, the Five Accounts, and Goal Setting for the Future, you are beginning to become acquainted with the benefits of growing financial strength. For example you should have a cash reserve fund, so you are no longer gripped by terror when your tires need replacing. Those kinds of typical "emergencies" are covered. You can afford to see into the future a little farther. At this point it may even dawn on you that you could be headed for wealth. We say, "could be" because many people choose to stop their money journey after financial independence is attained. If you don't stop you will become wealthy—you have built a well-oiled machine, and unless you flip the switch, it will keep on going and going and going. So prepare yourself to receive wealth. Wealth involves having more than a margin. Wealth is having a surplus, which means your wealth will take on a life of its own and outlive you.

In our culture we have a long list of fears and misconceptions about wealth. It's true that on the one hand, most of us have dreamed of having "lots of money," and we may have dreamed about what we would do if we won the lottery. By now we know why most lottery winners set about losing it as fast as they can. The fact is they are not prepared for wealth. Part of the purpose of the strategies outlined in this book is to prepare you for wealth so that when it arrives, you will not be intimidated or frightened by it, but will be ready to be wealthy. *The most important preparation for wealth is to transform your thinking regarding wealth.* Let's take a look at some of the myths that might hold you back.

Common myths about wealth are:
1. You will be a slave to your wealth. Your wealth will be too much to take care of and you will have to meet with your broker/banker every day.
2. Wealth will turn you into a corrupt, power-mad, greedy individual, and all the people you care about will leave you.
3. In the interest of saving your soul, God will be forced to rain down misfortune upon you.
4. Your children will be spoiled.
5. People will pester you constantly because they want your money.

6. No one will like you because you have money.
7. Everyone will only like you for your money.
8. If you are wealthy, it is at the expense of other people. There is not enough to go around.
9. Wealthy people have to engage in really boring social activities — no more bowling!
10. Money is evil.
11. You have to work *really hard* to become wealthy.
12. Men are the best money managers.
13. If you start too late, you can't get rich.
14. If you are a woman: "If I can't take care of myself, someone else will do it for me." This also shows up in the belief that if a woman is rich, she will be all alone, and paradoxically, if a woman is alone (without a man), she will be poor.

These statements really are myths. Let's look at them one by one.

1. *You will be a slave to your wealth.*

Many wealthy people do hire experts to manage their wealth. And, they probably spend less time meeting with them than you did figuring out how to get the money to pay for your car repairs, buy a suitable Valentine's gift without maxing out your credit card, and pay your bills every month. More time is not required; it is simply used in a different way.

2. Wealth will turn you into a corrupt, power-mad, greedy individual, and all the people you care about will leave you.

There are many poor people who are corrupt, power-mad, and greedy. These options are open to everyone. Money will only reveal the character that is already present. Poor people also get divorced, lose friends, and don't speak to their children. These situations do not come about simply because of money.

3. In the interest of saving your soul, God will be forced to rain down misfortune upon you.

Go to the county hospital. You will see poor people in misfortune. Unfortunate people can be found in every walk of life. A wealthy person has the advantage of taking care of expenses that accompany misfortune. A poor person doesn't have the same options.

4. Your children will be spoiled.

Spoiled children are not a direct result of having wealth. The boundaries of the parents are a much more powerful factor in determining whether a child will be well brought up or spoiled. There are many spoiled, out of control children in every socio-economic group.

5. *People will pester you constantly because they want your money.*

Being poor is not an effective protection against the demands of other people. No matter where you are in life, you need adequate boundaries. Boundaries are necessary to attain and retain wealth. Personal boundaries define you as a person separate from others. Boundaries protect and define; they keep good things in and bad things out. They keep peace between nations, neighbors and relatives. Boundaries protect your money from being at the mercy of other peoples' emergencies. They allow you to be the decision-maker for your money.

6. *No one will like you because you have money.*

This myth is what keeps people poor, stupid, drunk, and drug-addicted. The excessive need for approval will stop you from doing anything in life. Developing a strong sense of self is necessary to attain and retain wealth.

7. *Everyone will only like you for your money.*

This is simply another manifestation of the excessive need for approval. No matter what your financial state is, you have no control over what anybody thinks about you—period.

8. *If you are wealthy, it is at the expense of other people. There is not enough to go around.*

There truly is more than enough to go around. The acceptance of this statement may require a major transformation in your thinking. A number of books have been written about this. Some of our favorites are: *God Wants You To Be Rich, The Science of Getting Rich,* and *The Seven Spiritual Laws of Success*. If you remain poor, will people in India have more to eat? Will your family have more if you have less? The obvious answer is no. This is simply a myth. In fact, the more fulfilled and successful you become, the more the people you come in contact with will benefit as well. Start looking at the way things really work. Become a money scientist.

9. *Wealthy people have to engage in really boring social activities — no more bowling!*

Wealthy people have more options to do what they really want to do. Just because you can afford to play polo doesn't mean you won't still like bowling!

10. *Money is evil.*

The actual quote is: "The *love* of money is the root of all evil," which is quite different from "Money is the root of all evil." Money itself is neither good nor evil. Money is a tool. Giving the possession of money more importance than right values is what leads us into trouble. Making choices about money requires taking personal responsibility. If you think you are not making choices, think again. You are constantly making choices — by the way, you have made a choice to read this book — so you are going in the right direction!

11. *You have to work <u>really hard</u> to become wealthy.*

The truth is that your efforts to become wealthy have a cumulative effect. What you did two years ago pays off then, now, and five years from now. The fruit of your efforts grows and almost takes on a life of its own. Living in poverty is what demands really hard work. Poverty is actually the most expensive and grueling system on earth to maintain.

12. *Men are the best money managers.*

The truth is any person can learn to be a good money manager.

13. *If you start too late, you can't get rich.*

While it is advisable to begin saving and investing at a young age because it puts the power of time on your side, many people become wealthy in a matter of years. If you are an older person and you have decided to become wealthy, you may not have as many years as a 25-year old, but you are probably more focused, more savvy, and less distracted. You also have options a young person may not have. You are not trying to set up a household, raise children, or figure out what you are supposed to do with your life. Many wealthy people did not become successful until they were much older.

14. *If you are a woman: "If I can't take care of myself, someone else will do it for me." This also shows up in the belief that if a woman is rich, she will be all alone, and paradoxically, if a woman is alone (without a man), she will be poor.*

If a woman gets rich, she will have the option to fund the kind of life she wants with or without a man. As far as being helpless in order to get someone to take care of you — this may have worked during a certain period of childhood, but people who cannot take care of themselves when they get older usually get sent to the nursing home. Many women seem to have a particular problem with this myth. While this myth still survives within our culture, the truth is women who wait to be taken care of are often disappointed.

Now, let's talk about why you should want to be wealthy. Wealth expands and opens up possibilities in your life. For each person this will mean something different. One person may choose to build a special sunroom for their cats. One person may choose to travel. One person may choose to help a friend or family member to do something they really want to do. Just because you are wealthy doesn't mean you have to have a totally different lifestyle. Wealth will simply enable you to do more of what you already like to do. It will also allow you to do things that were formerly impossible to you that you would really like to be able to do.

Wealth also gives you power to do good. There are many organizations funded by wealthy people that benefit humanity. Wealth allows you to go beyond fulfilling your own needs and desires to contributing significantly to other people. Have you ever wanted to give money to a worthy cause and been forced to say no because you simply didn't have the money at the time? Imagine saying yes! Also, you get to take fabulous trips and see things you would not see otherwise! In short, wealth opens numerous doors and allows you to spread the joy. If you choose to continue on the money journey, you will need to lighten your load by leaving behind the excess baggage of myths about wealth.

Using Money to Reshape Your Life

~Chapter 10~
Becoming Debt Free

**"The fear of going too far keeps us from going far enough."
-- Sam Keen**

There are two schools of thought about paying off your debts. One says to just "get rich" and then pay off your debts. In other words, your money and energy should be going into investments. The profit from the investments will then be used to pay off debts and reinvest for more profit. The other school says to first pay off all your debts, including the mortgage, and *then* use the freed up income to invest for wealth. A strong case could be made for the "invest first, pay off your debts second" approach to wealth building, but we are not sold on this approach, and here is why: you need to have sufficient strength and resources to deal with the inevitable challenges that will arise with your wealth building efforts. If you have strength and resources you will be just fine. If you don't, you will be like a person with a compromised immune system walking into an infectious disease ward.

We believe in building wealth bit by bit. This approach allows you to create a solid foundation and to learn to maintain it during life's storms. Continue working on the strategies outlined in Chapter Six and the Five Accounts in Chapter Eight. Although it has taken some time, you have probably paid off some unsecured debts. It is now time to become totally debt free. At this point you should have a cash reserve fund for expenses that do not occur monthly; you should also be using cash and putting money in your five accounts.

Now it is time to pay off all your debts including your mortgage if you have one. Some of the books in the appendix explain different methods of accelerating your mortgage payoff. The point we'd like to make is that you can get your mortgage paid off much faster than 30 years, and it isn't that difficult to do. Like everything else in this book, it takes commitment. We believe in paying all debts, including the cars and mortgage as quickly as possible.

When you are completely debt free, you can withstand changes in your financial life much more than if you are still making house and car payments. If you had a sudden decrease in your income, and your house was paid for, you would only need to pay for current expenses. The lower your necessary monthly expenses, the more options you have to deal with life on every level.

You may be in agreement about getting out of debt. In fact, you may even be enthusiastic about the idea. Or you may be thinking, "It's a good idea but I just don't see how I could do it." Whatever your current feelings are about getting out of debt, we are here to tell you it really *can* be done. However, before you charge ahead into debt freedom, there are some things to consider about how you got into debt and how you have used debt in your life. Consider the following possibilities:

1. Debt does provide a plan and structure for the future and relieves you of the anxiety of making financial decisions every month. Your money has already been spent before you get your paycheck, relieving you of the responsibility of making decisions. Sometimes the idea of being responsible for finances is so anxiety producing that you may find yourself gladly relinquishing control. Of course, this is hardly ever a good idea. If you are on the road to debt freedom be willing to take back control of your finances.

2. Debt connects you to your past and relieves you from the anxiety of planning for your future. As long as you have debt, it is hard to move into your future or even to envision your future. Also, there may be something in your past you are attempting to resolve. For example, if you are divorced and paying off debts that were incurred while you were married, you may keep the debt going in an attempt to resolve unfinished business in your marriage. Debt may connect you to a failed marriage or a happier time. It may also allow you to continue a lifestyle you once

enjoyed but that has become too costly to maintain. It can keep you in the past and shield you from unpleasant realities in the present.

3. Debt can be a way to connect to a type of family structure. You may feel that your credit card is your emergency fund. The credit card company will bail you out if you need help, just like mother did when you were in college and ran out of money. Debt can give you a certain feeling of safety, especially when you are not sure you can handle things on your own.

4. Debt can protect you from invasive family and friends who are continually making demands on your finances. Many of these demands are very hard to say no to because they are presented as an emergency. There is often a spoken or implied statement such as "If I had the money, I would help you." What we know deep down is that this person will never have the money so will never have to make good on that promise. Being in debt means all your money is spoken for. Debt creates a boundary between you and the needy person that effectively protects you from unending demands. Debt gives you the opportunity to say, "Gosh, I don't have the money either. But if I did have the money, I'd help you too." If this is the situation in which you find

yourself, our advice to you is—don't tell the needy person you are planning on getting out of debt. Your finances are your business—not anyone else's. The first line of defense is don't give out any information. If someone asks you for information, be vague. It is not necessary for you to give out personal information just because someone has asked.

5. Debt allows you to live with gusto and consume mass quantities. It allows you to spend more than you have. Spending less than you earn may not sound very glamorous but it does give you a peaceful feeling because you know your finances are stable and getting stronger, not weaker. Also, once you have saved some of your own money, you can loan it out to yourself and pay yourself back. It's just like having a credit card. Only it is zero percent forever and you never have to call about your statement.

After you are completely debt free, you have the option of wealth building with a vengeance. There are many books on wealth building, and it is not the purpose of this book to lie out a specific strategy. At this point, your five accounts will assume even greater importance. The five accounts train you to understand the functions of money and how all of the functions work together to build and sustain wealth. The Annual Income Account holds cash reserves. The Investment Account makes money that is to be divided between the other accounts. The sole purpose of the Financial Independence Account is to amass principal—the idea being that at some point, you will be able to live off the interest. The Spending Account provides a balance in your money system since you must spend all of the money in this account. Are you starting to understand that the functions of money go beyond simply spending or saving?

It is important to build a balanced money structure. You need a cushion (Annual Income Account), the money earmarked for creating wealth (Investment Account), and money to enjoy (Spending Account). Yes! One of the purposes of money is for enjoyment! You also need to have an understanding that there is more than enough money for your needs and wants, (Financial Independence Account). The Financial Independence Account will also help you to change from being a weak ineffectual person to a strong soon to be wealthy person who is amassing a principal sum. If you concentrate on only one of the functions of money, your system will be lopsided and will not function efficiently. You may choose to work one function more intensely than the others after all your accounts have been opened. This is fine in the beginning. You will be working with new concepts that may require time and effort to assimilate. As time passes the structure itself will help you to develop balance in your finances.

Being debt free is a much simpler and more peaceful way to live. Putting money in the Five Accounts keeps you grounded, balanced, and open to attracting more money and opportunities. Paying interest on a credit card may help the credit card company, but it doesn't help you. Being debt free gives you the opportunity to build wealth.

Using Money to Reshape Your Life

~Conclusion~

Supposing you have tried and failed again and again. You may have a fresh start any moment you choose, for this thing that we call "failure" is not the falling down, but the staying down. -- Mary Pickford

We hope this book has helped you start to change your relationship with money. This is one of the most important relationships you will ever have in your life, so it is worth the trouble and discomfort it will take to make it peaceful. Using the strategies outlined in Chapter Six and the Five Accounts will help you gain control of your finances. If this process takes awhile, don't fret. It is worth it. We hope our experiences have helped you.

Using Money to Reshape Your Life

~Book and Tape List~

These are the books and tapes we read together. This is a limited list, however. We are still reading and hope you will avail yourself of the hundreds of books, tapes, and publications that are available.

Books

- Avanzini, John. *Rapid Debt Reduction Strategies.* Hurst, TX: HIS Publishing Company, 1990.
- Beardstown Ladies Investment Club with Leslie Whitaker. *The Beardstown Ladies Common Sense Investment Guide.* New York: Hyperion, 1994.
- Beavis, Wes. *Escape to Prosperity.* Los Angeles: Powerborn, 1999.
- Belsky, Gary and Thomas Gilovich. *Why Smart People Make Big Money Mistakes – and How to Correct Them: Lessons from the New Science of Behavioral Economics.* New York: Simon & Schuster, 1999.
- Cameron, Julia and Mark Bryan. *The Artist's Way: A Spiritual Path to Higher Creativity.* New York: G. P. Putnam Sons, 1992.

- Cameron, Julia. *The Vein of Gold: A Journey to Your Creative Heart.* New York: G. P. Putnam Sons, 1996.
- Chilton, David. *The Wealthy Barber: Everyone's Common-Sense Guide to Becoming Financially Independent.* Prima Publishing, 1996.
- Chopra, Deepak. *The Seven Spiritual Laws of Success: A Practical Guide to the Fulfillment of Your Dreams.* San Rafael, CA: Amber-Allen Publishing; Novato, CA: New World Library, 1994.
- Csikszentmihalyi, Mihaly. *Flow: The Psychology of Optimal Experience.* New York: HarperPerennial, 1991.
- Csilszentmihalyi, Mihaly. *Creativity: Flow and the Psychology of Invention.* New York: Harper Perennial, 1996.
- Dacyczyn, Amy. *The Tightwad Gazette: Promoting Thrift as a Viable Lifestyle, vol.I,II,III.* New York: Villard Books, 1993.
- Pollan, Stephen M. and Mark Levine. *Die Broke: A Radical, Four-Part Financial Plan to Restore Your Confidence, Increase Your Net Worth, and Afford You the Lifestyle of Your Dreams.* New York: Harper Business, 1997.
- Dominguez, Joe, and Vicki Robin. *Your Money or Your Life: Transforming Your Relationship with Money and Achieving Financial Independence.* New York: Penguin Books, 1992.
- Elgin, Duane. *Voluntary Simplicity: Toward a Way of Life That is Outwardly Simple, Inwardly Rich.* New York: Quill, A Division of William Morrow, 1993.
- Gardner, David and Tom. *The Motley Fool Investment Workbook.* New York: Fireside, 1998.

- Gunther, Max. *The Luck Factor: Why Some People are Luckier Than Others and How You Can Become One of Them.* New York: Macmillan Publishing Company, Inc., 1977.
- Hill, Napoleon *Think and Grow Rich.* New York: Fawcett Crest, 1960.
- Kiyosaki, Robert T., and Sharon L. Lechter, C.P.A. *Rich Dad, Poor Dad: What the Rich Teach Their Kids About Money – That The Poor And Middle Class Do Not!* New York: Warner Books, 1998.
- Laut, Phil. *Money is My Friend: Eliminate your Financial Fears – and Take Your First Steps to Financial Freedom.* New York: Ballantine Books, 1990.
- Laut, Phil, and Andy Fuehl. Wealth *Without a Job: The Entrepreneur's Guide to Freedom and Security Beyond the 9 to 5 Lifestyle.* New Jersey: John Wiley & Sons, Inc., 2004.
- Madenes, Cloe, with Claudio Madenes. *The Secret Meaning of Money: How it Binds Together Families in Love, Envy, Compassion, or Anger.* San Francisco: Jossey-Bass Publishers, 1994.
- Moore, John. *Conscious Prosperity: The Secret to Simple and Lasting Personal Wealth.* Clearwater Beach, Florida: Creating Wealth Workshop, 2002.
- Orman, Suze. *The Nine Steps to Financial Freedom: Practical and Spiritual Steps so You Can Stop Worrying.* New York: Crown Publishers, Inc., 1997.

- Pilzer, Paul Zane. *God Wants You to Be Rich: How and Why Everyone Can Enjoy Material and Spiritual Wealth in Our Abundant World.* New York: Fireside, 1997.
- Proctor, Bob. *You Were Born Rich.* Georgia: Life Success Productions, 1997.
- Ramsey, Dave. *Financial Peace: Putting Common Sense into your Dollars and Sense.* Nashville: Lampo Press, 1995.
- Stanley, Thomas J., and William Danko. *The Millionaire Next Door: The Surprising Secrets of America's Wealthy.* New York: Simon & Schuster, 1996.
- Thoreau, Henry David. *Walden.* New York: A Signet Classic published by The Penguin Group.
- Wattles, Wallace D. *The Science of Getting Rich.* Georgia: Life Success Productions, 1996.
- Vitale, Joe. *The Attractor Factor: 5 Easy Steps for Creating Wealth (or Anything Else) From the Inside Out.* New Jersey: John Wiley & Sons, Inc., 2005.
- Zander, Rosamund Stone and Benjamin Zander. *The Art of Possibility: Transforming Professional and Personal Life.* Boston, Mass: Harvard Business School Press, 2000.

Tapes

Lehrman, Fredric. *Prosperity Consciousness: How to Tap Your Unlimited Wealth.* Nightingale-Conant Corporation, 1-800-325-5552.

Visit Us at our Websites
www.financiallyhopelessnomore.com
www.dare2dreambooks.com

To Contact Us or for Information or Comments
e-mail Courtney and Lynn at
financiallyhopelessnomore@gmail.com

or e-mail the publisher at
dare2dreambooks@yahoo.com

Printed in the United States
85541LV00001B/52-150/A